a work of art

Joan Chambers, Molly Hood and Michael Peake

NATALIA

Line drawings by Michael Peake

First Published in 1995 by
BELAIR PUBLICATIONS LIMITED
P.O. Box 12, Twickenham, England, TW1 2QL

© 1995 Joan Chambers, Molly Hood and Michael Peake
Series Editor Robyn Gordon
Designed by Richard Souper
Photography by Kelvin Freeman
Typesetting by Belair
Printed and Bound in Hong Kong through World Print Ltd
ISBN 0 947882 58 8

Acknowledgements

The Authors and Publishers would like to thank the following children for their special contributions to the artwork: Louise Borg, Alexandra Chambers, Stephen Chambers, Marie Clarke, Katie Garlick, Katherine Giles, Graeme Goulson, Lee Hawkes, Lucy Hellings, Emma Hunter, Bartek Jablonski, Michal Jabonski, Gemma Satchell, Natalie Thompson and Richard Thompson.

They would also like to thank Douglas Chambers for his invaluable assistance, and Kay Hoskins for contributing the creative writing.

Special thanks to Alexandra Chambers for the cover artwork.

Scratch-back picture inspired by Paul Klee

The cover picture is an interpretation of *Irises* by Vincent Van Gogh

Contents

Introduction

Welcome to *A Work of Art.* This book is intended to stimulate children's creativity by introducing them to some of the works of great artists. The paintings are used as starting points for a variety of creative activities.

● Many of the ideas based on one artist can be readily adapted for other artists, and can also be used on their own for single art lessons.

● We have included ideas for various ages which can often be adapted for use across the age range.

● All of the sections include photographs of children's art inspired by famous artists. Many sections also include a print of the artist's work.

● There are many suggestions for the display of children's artwork, and ideas to encourage older children to create new ways to present their own work.

● Some background information on each artist is given, which can be supplemented by the many books and art packs currently available.

● The wide range of historical periods and artistic styles will encourage discussion and comparison.

● We have found that children are inspired by using interesting materials, with freedom to experiment.

We hope that children will enjoy learning about the artists, looking at the pictures, and using these as inspiration for their own works of art.

Joan Chambers, Molly Hood and Michael Peake

Giotto di Bondone (c.1266-1337)

Giotto was born in a small village in Italy called Mugello. There is a story told that the famous artist Cimabue was passing the village and admired the drawings of sheep that a little shepherd boy had made on a rock to pass the time. That little boy was Giotto, and the artist invited him to join his studio. He went on to become more famous than his teacher. Giotto based his paintings on real people and places, and became famous for making the people in his paintings so lifelike.

St Francis Honoured by a Simple Man, 1296-97, by Giotto, Ambrogio Bondone, (c.1266-1337)
S. Francesco, Upper Church, Assisi/Bridgeman Art Library, London

This is one of a series of frescoes about the life of St Francis of Assisi, who gave up all his wealth to live a simple life of service to the poor. He became the patron saint of animals and birds - he said they were his brothers and sisters. The designs are thought to be by Giotto because of the natural expressions and positions of the figures. Frescoes are completed in sections, because they have to be painted when the plaster is still wet. It took a whole day to paint the saint's head. Each panel in the series shows a different story about St. Francis, and you can still see the buildings and the landscape if you visit Assisi today. The Temple of Minerva in the picture is still there, but in reality it has six pillars, not five.

ST. FRANCIS FRESCO
Materials:
Blue paper for background
Pieces of paper in pink, green, white
Chalks in pink, green, brown, blue, white
Scissors, glue

1. Look at Giotto's fresco on the previous page.
2. Using the side of a piece of blue chalk, rub over the blue paper to create the effect of a fresco.
3. Draw and cut out the shapes of the buildings and rub over them with the other coloured chalks. Draw in details.
4. Repeat with the figures, and glue on to the background.
5. Cut some strips of white paper and decorate with chalk to make borders.

WOOD PANELS
Religious paintings were often painted on wooden panels, linked together to make diptychs (two panels), triptychs (three panels), and polyptychs (four or more panels). Frequently, they were hinged so that they could be closed.

Look at the photograph to see the different shapes, and then design your own folding version. Use a variety of materials including card, gold spray, paint or pen, thick felt-tip pens, pencils, etc. Make a modern version and add figures from a religious story. Find a picture of Giotto's *Bologna Polyptych* if possible, and see how he made the figures fit the archway shapes.

DECORATIVE MOTIFS

Giotto often painted elaborate borders around fresco paintings. The patterns on this page come from his designs in the Scrovegni Chapel in Padua. In the panels he painted scenes from the Bible, or portraits of saints.

Photocopy these motifs and decorate to make bookmarks.

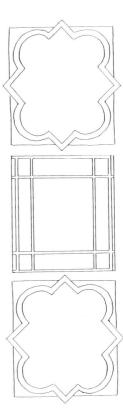

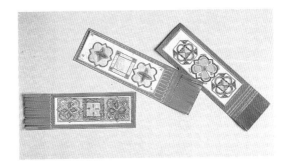

CIRCLES

When Giotto was asked by the Pope to prove he was a great artist, he simply drew a perfect circle, freehand. The Pope was convinced. Here are some ways of drawing circles. Do them in pencil first, correct them, and go over them with pen or felt-tip pen.

- Draw a dot first for the centre of the circle and repeat as above.
- Start drawing a straight line and, without stopping, curve the line around to make a circle.
- Draw a dot for the centre and then draw a number of dots which are all the same distance from the centre one. Join all the outside dots to make a circle.
- Draw a square. Draw a dot at the mid-point of each side. Join the dots with curved lines to make a circle.

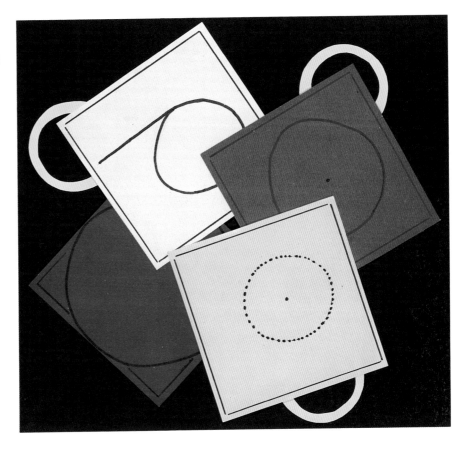

Simone Martini (1284-1344)

Simone Martini was probably born in Siena, Italy. It was such a long time ago that very little is known of his life. In those days, to become an artist meant learning the trade in a workshop which was run by a master painter. Workshops often had members of the same family painting together. Martini painted with his brother and his brother-in-law, Lippi Memmi. Later in life he was knighted because of his beautiful paintings. This was very unusual for an artist and it was a great honour for him. The Church in the Middle Ages was very powerful and wealthy, and was the main patron of art. Most of Martini's paintings are religious scenes, painted for the walls and altars of churches and monasteries.

Guidoriccio da Fogliano at the Siege of Montemassi (fresco) by Simone Martini (1284-1344), Palazzo Publicco, Siena / Bridgeman Art Library, London

This fresco, attributed to Simone Martini, is on the wall of the town hall in Siena. It celebrates the conquest of the Castle of Montemassi in 1328. The castle is towards the right in the picture. In the centre is Guidoriccio da Fogliano, riding triumphantly towards the town. Underneath the fresco is the date MCCCXXVIII, which is the date of the victory.

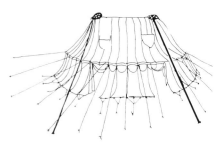

Tent

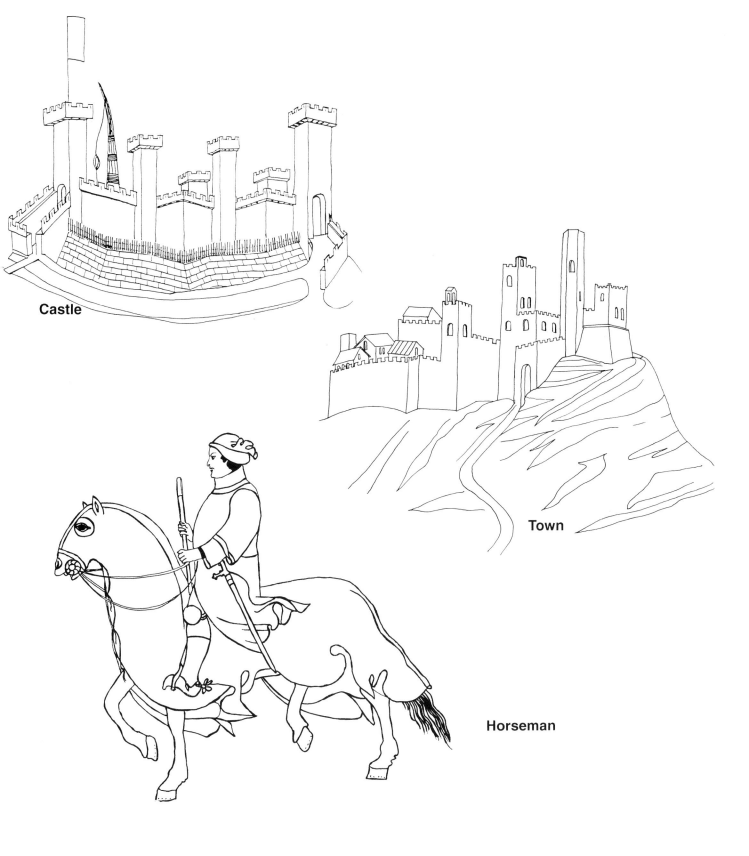

Castle

Town

Horseman

There are four main images of the picture shown on the facing page - town, knight, castle and camp. Use these outlines to create your own wall-painting. Enlarge or reduce as desired on a photocopier. Make your own design for the horseman and his horse. Decorate the man's clothing first, and then repeat the pattern on the horse.

Sandro Botticelli (1444/5-1510)

The painter we know as Botticelli was really Alessandro di Mariano di Vanni Filipepi. He took his name from his brother's nickname 'Botticello', meaning *little barrel.* When he was a young boy he asked his father if he could join the workshop of Fra Filippo Lippi, a famous painter in the town of Florence where they lived. The boy learnt very quickly, and by the time he was 25 he had his own workshop in Florence and had become as famous as his teacher. He painted many pictures for his patron, who was one of the Medici family. He also painted pictures for the Pope. People admired him particularly for the beautiful and graceful way he drew the figures in his paintings.

Many of Botticelli's paintings were intended for churches, so they have religious subjects such as *Madonna and Child,* or *The Nativity.* He was painting in Italy during the period we call the *Renaissance,* which means 're-birth'. This was a time of exciting new ideas, many inspired by Ancient Greek and Roman art and writings. Botticelli painted many pictures of ancient myths and legends - for example, *Mars and Venus* and *Primavera.*

Madonna of the Magnificat by Sandro Botticelli (1444/5 -1510),
Galleria degli Uffizi, Florence / Bridgeman Art Library, London

This painting (c.1485) is one of Botticelli's most famous. These round pictures are called *tondos,* and the beautiful figures were painted to follow the circular shape. Note how the window in the painting is rounded. The title of the painting comes from the name of a prayer, 'The Magnificat', the first word of which appears on the book in the picture. Many of the fine details have been added in gold paint.

FRAMED DETAILS

One way of looking at a painting is to concentrate on a section or a small detail. Choose a detail from the picture on the facing page and make your own picture.

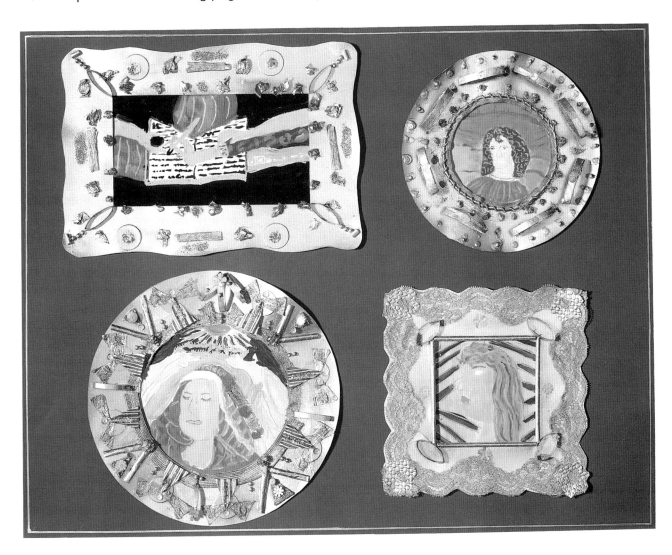

Materials

Thin card for background
Frames cut from thin card in various
   shapes, e.g. square, rectangular,
   round or oval
Felt-tip pens
Paints, pencil
Small brushes

Scraps of collage materials, e.g.
   card, polystyrene, beads, leaves,
   straws, lace, flower shapes cut
   from cardboard
Gold spray or paint
Strong glue, scissors

1. Place the frame on the background and draw lightly with a pencil around the inside of the frame. Remove frame and draw inside the shape.
2. Using the pencil, draw a detail from the picture, for example, head, book, Madonna.
3. Paint the picture using similar colours to the original.
4. Decorate the frame with collage materials in a symmetrical pattern.
5. When dry, paint or spray the frame with gold paint, and glue on to the picture.

● Collect pictures or photographs of adults in your family. Write about these and design your own frames for them.
● Find some paintings of babies. Discuss the different ways they were painted.

THE GODDESS OF SPRING

Botticelli painted many pictures based on myths and legends, for example, *The Birth of Venus.* Some also represented a season in human form, as in *Primavera,* (the Goddess of Spring).

Draw your own figure to represent Summer, Autumn, Winter or Spring.
Make a background with coloured tissue paper using appropriate colours for one of the seasons. Fold the surplus over at the back and glue down to make a neat edge.
Decorate the figure using tissue paper and paint. Glue it on to the background.

Frame: Cut a rectangular frame from gold card. Decorate with any of the following gold-coloured materials - ribbon, lace, card, doily, beads, paper, sequins. If gold materials are not available, use other scraps painted gold. When dry, cut a wavy pattern around the edge.

LOGGIA

Many Renaissance buildings had loggias attached to them. These were open-air galleries which often had colonnades (rows of columns) or arcades (rows of arches). Many were used to display Greek and Roman statues.

Make a photocopy of a picture of a loggia or draw your own. The model of the loggia in the photograph is based on the one in the Piazza della Signoria in Florence. Cut out the photocopy and glue on to a cereal box the same size. Cut out the arches and paint the box to make the loggia. Photocopy or draw classical statues to fit inside the arches. Glue these on to card and mount on cardboard pedestals and place inside the loggia.

RENAISSANCE PALACE DISPLAY

The interiors of Italian palaces were often very ornate, with rich furnishings, beautiful paintings and sculptures.

Display idea: Create a corner of an Italian palace. Collect pieces of fabric, such as velvet, damask and silk in deep colours. Old photograph frames could be painted or sprayed with gold paint. Find postcards or pictures by Renaissance artists. Some objects to include in this display are candlesticks, jewellery, ornate boxes, mirrors, goblets, statues, or any other suitable ornaments.

JEWEL BOXES

Cover a small box with two layers of tissue paper in strong colours, for example, purple, red, royal blue, silver or gold. Cover the lower part of the box first and the lid last. Decorate with patterns using gold and silver pens, or shiny materials.

WOODCUT

Early books were often illustrated with woodcuts - a type of printing.
The woodcut shown here originally contained a portrait of Botticelli (as shown on page 70). The details on the frame show that Botticelli was an artist.

Photocopy this woodcut using an enlargement facility and add a profile drawing of a friend, or yourself. This can be used as a book-plate (see Title page). Write a name in the panel and add serifs as shown on the Title page. Design your own book-plate with details to show your hobbies and interests.

NATALIA

Leonardo da Vinci (1452-1519)

Leonardo da Vinci was born in Vinci, a small country town in Italy. Very little is known about his childhood, but we know that he enjoyed painting and drawing when he was a boy. His father showed his drawings to a famous artist called Verrocchio, who asked da Vinci to join his workshop at the age of seventeen. At that time, it was the tradition for several painters to work on the same picture, each doing a different part. Only a few of his wonderful paintings have survived, the most famous being the *Mona Lisa*.

Da Vinci was very curious about nature and science, and was always experimenting, studying and making observations in his notebooks. He was left-handed and wrote in mirror writing because he wanted to keep his ideas secret. He was a genius who was gifted in many areas. As well as being a painter, he was an architect, sculptor, inventor and a brilliant musician.

Cartoon for Virgin and Child with St Anne by Leonardo da Vinci
(1452-1519), National Gallery, London / Bridgeman Art Library, London

Nowadays, the word *cartoon* means a comic drawing or an animated film. Originally, the word referred to a drawing done in preparation for a painting (see Glossary). Da Vinci drew this cartoon when planning a painting for a monastery. People came from miles around to see the drawing, but unfortunately da Vinci never managed to complete the painting.
The picture shows the Virgin Mary and her mother, St Anne, with Jesus and the young John the Baptist.

A LEONARDO DA VINCI DISPLAY

Create a display to show the range of Da Vinci's abilities and interests. Da Vinci planned many inventions, for example, the parachute and the helicopter.
Some other things to include are portraits, sketches from nature (for example, shells and plants), weapons and the human body.

- Write out the alphabet. Hold it in front of a mirror and copy out the reversed alphabet that you can see. Use this as a code to write secret messages.
- Make sketches with a pencil on cream or beige paper. Go over the drawing with a fine-line pen. Try using other drawing media, for example, red or black chalk on pale pink paper. Highlight with white chalk.
- Decorate the edges of pictures and writing with gold felt-tip pen and mount on dark red, gold or dark blue.

A LETTER TO THE DUKE

Da Vinci once wanted to work for the Duke of Milan, and sent him a letter describing all the things he could do, for example, bridge-building, designing weapons for attacking fortresses and for fighting sea-battles, making covered chariots, designing ways of moving water from one place to another.

- Write your own letter to a famous person making a list of the wonderful things you can do. This can be as unbelievable as you like. Decorate your letter with some drawings.

Pieter Brueghel - the Elder (1525-1569)

Pieter Brueghel grew up in Holland in quite a wealthy family. His paintings were mainly of the countryside and its people. When he was a young man he went on a trip to Italy. He was amazed by the size and grandeur of the Swiss and Italian Alps, which were so different from the flat landscape of his native Holland. The mountains appear in many of his paintings and engravings.

Hunters in the Snow, by Pieter Brueghel, the Elder (c.1525-69), Gemaldegalerie, Kunsthistorisches Museum, Vienna/Bridgeman Art Library, London

This painting was one of a set of six, each representing two months of the year:

The Hay Harvest - June/July

The Return of the Herd - October/November

The Dark Day - February/March

The Wheat Harvest - August/September,

Hunters in the Snow - December/January

(No painting survives for April and May)

Although the painting looks like a real scene, it is imaginary. It combines the flat landscape of the Netherlands and its rivers, canals and villages, with the mountains that Brueghel had seen in Italy and Switzerland. The picture seems to have been painted from a high hilltop. On the hill close to us are the hunters and their dogs, which seem quite large. We look down on the vast landscape with lots of little villages dotted about. By making the figures and objects in the distance very small, Brueghel makes them seem further away.

WINTER LANDSCAPE

The picture on the right shows how to make the background for a wall display or a collage. This makes an ideal group activity.

Using coloured paper, draw and cut out some of the details from *Hunters in the Snow,* for example, figures, houses, trees, bridges, churches and animals. Make these in different sizes. Glue on to the background with the largest pieces in the foreground, and the smallest in the distance. Add details with felt-tip pens.

THREE-IN-ONE LANDSCAPE

Brueghel created an unusual effect by combining the flat landscape of Holland and the mountains of Switzerland and Italy in the same painting.

Make a list of types of landscapes, for example, desert, urban, mountainous, snowy, jungle. Combine three of these to make your own picture. If desired, add figures, using felt-tip pens.

William Hogarth (1697-1764)

Hogarth was born and grew up in London, the son of a school teacher. When he was young, all his free time was spent drawing, and even his school work was covered with decoration. From the age of 15 he was apprenticed to an engraver. He became a well-known portrait painter, but became even more famous for his scenes of everyday life.

Hogarth liked to tell a story in his paintings, and in the engravings he made from them. He painted many series of pictures which showed the evils in society, for example, greed and cruelty, and their consequences. His engravings are full of interesting and closely-observed details.

The Enraged Musician was designed and engraved by Hogarth, and published on November 30, 1741

The violinist in the picture wants to practise, but the noises in the street are so loud that he cannot hear himself play. What are the other noises in the street? Look for the knife-grinder, the postman blowing his horn, the milkmaid, the ballad singer, and the chimeysweep. What street sellers' cries can you hear nowadays (for example, newspaper sellers, market traders)?

HATCHING

Look at the way Hogarth created a range of tones from white to black, just by using lines (hatching). He used lines of different thicknesses and varied the spacing between them. To get a darker tone he used criss-cross lines (cross-hatching). Notice how he sometimes curved the lines to suggest the shape of, for example, the girl's bodice.

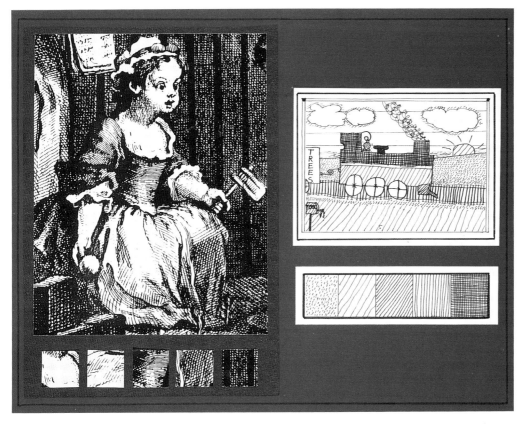

● Experiment with hatching by drawing a simple picture and filling in the shapes with lines.
● Enlarge one of the figures on the photocopier, either from *The Enraged Musician* or another Hogarth print. Draw your own figure using the same hatching techniques.

SOUND PICTURE

Make a list of sounds heard in the street. Draw a picture using felt-tip pens to represent as many of these as possible. Exchange your drawing with a partner and see how many sounds are represented in each of your pictures.

Joseph Mallord William Turner (1775-1851)

Turner lived most of his life in London. As a boy he loved to watch the bustle and activity on the river Thames. His fascination with ships appears in paintings like *The Fighting Temeraire.*

When he was young, his father hung his pictures on the walls of his barber's shop. A few years later, Turner's paintings were hanging on the walls of the Royal Academy of Art, the most important art school in England. He travelled widely in Britain and Europe, carrying a sketchbook wherever he went. Often he made his landscapes more dramatic by painting them as if he were looking directly at the sun.

When he died, Turner left 250 sketchbooks to the nation, 19,000 sketches and hundreds of watercolours and oil paintings.

Rain, Steam and Speed, The Great Western Railway, by Joseph Mallord William Turner (1775-1851), National Gallery, London / Bridgeman Art Library, London

This painting was so different from others of the time that an art critic encouraged the public 'to hasten to see the work lest the train should dash out of the picture and be away up Charing Cross through the wall opposite'.

Before Turner painted this picture, he took a train journey in the heavy rain, keeping his head out of the window for some time to get the effect of speed in wet weather. He painted a hare running in front of the engine to show the speed of the train.

BRIDGE IN THE MIST

Many of Turner's paintings have an atmosphere which suggests the weather, for example, *Rain, Steam and Speed* (see facing page).

Turner was always experimenting with different techniques. Often, when painting with watercolours, he tried scratching and scraping, wiping out, adding extra water and using white paint in washes and dabs.

Experiment by painting on different types of paper, for example, wallpaper, kitchen paper, etc. and using any of the materials below.

Materials:
Paper (for background)
Watercolour paints in various
    colours
Brushes
Pieces of sponge
Soft crumpled paper, cotton wool,
    tissues
Pencils, fine-line pens

1. Make a list of words suggested by the picture, for example, smoky, hazy, misty, stormy, drizzly, foggy, etc.
2. Using a pencil, draw part of a bridge on the paper. Also draw part of a boat, aeroplane or train somewhere else on the page.
3. Wet the paper with a sponge or brush and add large dabs of paint, allowing the colours to run into each other. Leave to dry.
4. Draw in details with the pens.

TURNER'S SKETCHBOOKS

Turner made sketches every day in his notebooks. He used pencil, chalk, paint or pen with different coloured inks.

Make your own sketchbook. Use pale blue paper, or paper tinted with a pale coloured wash, for example, beige. Draw and paint what you see around you during a single day - for example, your own possessions, things you do, people in your life, and games you like. Decorate the cover with pictures.

Katsushika Hokusai (1760-1849)

Kirifura Fall in Kurokawa Mountain, from the series 'A Journey to the Waterfalls of all the Provinces' ('Shokoku taki meguri') by Katsushika Hokusai (1760-1849), pub. by Nishimura Eijudo, c.1832, (hand-coloured woodblock print), Fitzwilliam Museum, University of Cambridge / Bridgeman Art Library, London

Hokusai was an artist from Japan whose works became famous all over the world. He was adopted by a mirror-polisher, who taught him his craft, and later he went on to learn woodblock carving. Eventually, he decided to design his own woodblock pictures. From the age of six Hokusai had a passion for drawing and painting. In his very long life, he produced 30,000 designs with many different subjects: landscapes, waterfalls, bridges, portraits of actors, beautiful women, birds, flowers, fish, and Japanese legends.

Here are two stories about Hokusai to show the sort of artist he was.
- Once he painted a gigantic picture of a Buddhist figure in front of a large crowd of people. The painting was so huge that he had to use brooms dipped in big bowls of ink for paint brushes. Only the people on top of a nearby building could see what he was painting.
- Another time he was commanded to paint in a competition in front of the Shogun (the virtual ruler of Japan). He painted the curves of a blue river on a large paper screen. Then he dipped the feet of a chicken in red paint and made it run all over the picture. He called the picture *Maple Leaves in Autumn Floating down the River.*

The waterfall shown on the facing page is a famous landmark on the way to the Toshogu Shrine at Nikko. Waterfall pictures can be created in many different ways, for example, using pastels, tissue paper or crêpe paper.

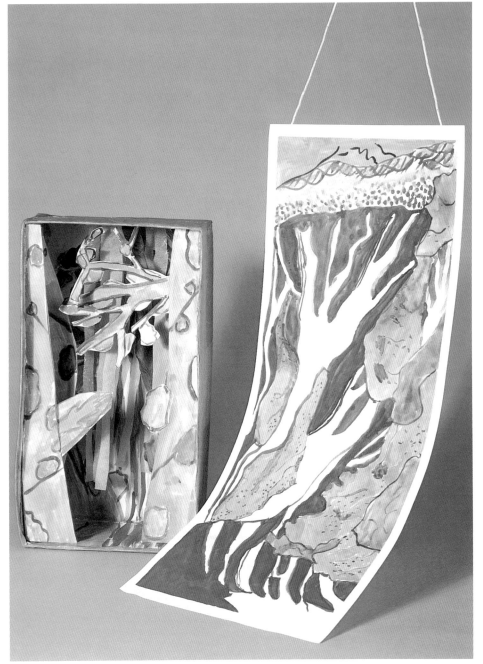

WATERFALL IN A BOX
Materials
Shoe box
Crêpe and tissue paper,
    white paper
Paint, thick brushes
Scraps of Cellophane
Scissors, glue

1. Look at a Hokusai waterfall picture.
2. Cover the outside of the box with blue or green tissue paper.
3. Decorate the back of the waterfall first with any of the materials above.
4. Paint trees and banks on the white paper. Cut these out and glue on to create a 3D view.

● Try this as a group activity to make a waterfall corner.

WATERFALL WALL-HANGING
Materials
Pale coloured paper for
    background
Paints, brushes

1. Cut a long, thin piece of paper to make the wall-hanging.
2. Draw a waterfall design in pencil. Notice how Hokusai shows part of a tree coming in at the edge of the picture.
3. The ends of the painting could be glued on to pieces of stick or bamboo, or rolled up to form a scroll. (In Japan, these long thin paintings were hung on pillars.)

● To give a rainy effect to a landscape, make slanted lines across the scene using a ruler and a pencil or a fine pen.
● Hokusai designed a famous series of prints called *Thirty-six Views of Mount Fuji.* Choose a local landmark and make your own series based on this.
● Hokusai painted a picture called *'100 bridges'.* Design your own version of this and see how many types of bridges you could include. Add roads and pathways linking them.

Japanese fans came in two main styles. One was circular and did not fold. The other one folded, and when opened out was the shape of the ones in the photograph. Japanese artists made woodblock prints for both types.

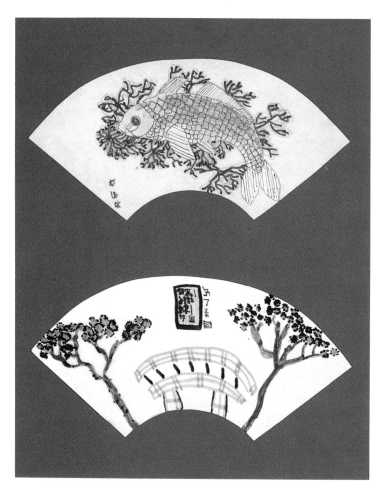

JAPANESE FANS
Materials:
White paper
Piece of tissue paper in pale colours, larger than the above
Pencil, felt-tip pens
Scissors and glue

1. Draw a fan shape on the white paper (or photocopy and enlarge fan shape from the photograph).
2. Cut this out. Cover with tissue paper and glue the surplus on to the back.
3. Draw a Japanese design, for example, fish, lanterns, flowers or landscape, with pencil, and decorate with felt-tip pens.

HOKUSAI DRAWINGS
These drawings are based on details from Hokusai prints. Use these or details from other Hokusai prints to make your own Japanese landscape. Paint a watercolour background and, when dry, add details with a fine-line pen.

MT FUJI

The original print by Hokusai is called *Fuji in Clear Weather.* It was produced in 1823 and was part of the series called *Thirty-six Views of Mt Fuji.* Mt Fuji is a beautiful and much loved landmark in Japan.

Try some of these different ways of representing Mt Fuji.

- **Printing.** Draw and cut out the shape of Mt Fuji using a piece of thin polystyrene or card. Cover this with red paint, and print on to a blue background. Print the trees and clouds using scraps of polystyrene, dipped in green and white paint.
- **Greetings Card.** Using watercolours, draw and paint a Mt Fuji scene on a small piece of paper. Glue on to a piece of folded card.
- **Tissue Paper Collage.** Cover a piece of paper with blue tissue paper and fold the surplus over on to the back. Make a collage picture using pieces of coloured paper.

● Make a picture of Mt Fuji in other weather conditions, for example, rain, snow, storm, mist.
● Make your own series, changing the size and position of Mt Fuji, and introducing different foregrounds, for example, cherry blossoms, trees, temples, bridges.
● Find a picture of Hokusai's famous print, *The Great Wave.* Note how small Mt Fuji appears. Make your own wave picture.

John Everett Millais (1829-1896)

Millais came from the Channel Islands. He was so gifted that he was accepted at the Royal Academy of Art in London when he was only 11 years old, and he became the most brilliant student of his day. Millais' pictures often told a simple story and showed a very close observation of nature. He formed a group with some other artists and they called themselves *the Pre-Raphaelite Brotherhood.* They created a new style of art, inspired by early Italian painters. Their subjects were frequently based on medieval legends. Eventually Millais became very wealthy and famous. When he was older, he changed his style and painted very popular pictures of children. One of these, *Bubbles,* became famous as an advertisement for a soap company.

Ophelia, 1851-52, by Sir John Everett Millais (1829-96), Tate Gallery, London / Bridgeman Art Library, London

This painting shows Ophelia, a character in Shakespeare's play *Hamlet.* She is seen floating in the stream and singing, after she had fallen into the water while picking flowers. To paint the river scene, Millais spent many weeks in summer sitting under an umbrella beside the Hogsmill River near Ewell in Surrey.

In the winter, he worked in his studio to complete the picture. The model for Ophelia was a girl called Lizzy Siddal. Every day for four months she lay in a bath in her silver gown. Millais kept lamps burning under the tub to keep the water warm. One day he let the lamps go out and Lizzy caught a cold. Her father made Millais pay the doctor's bill. Fortunately Lizzy recovered.

OPHELIA

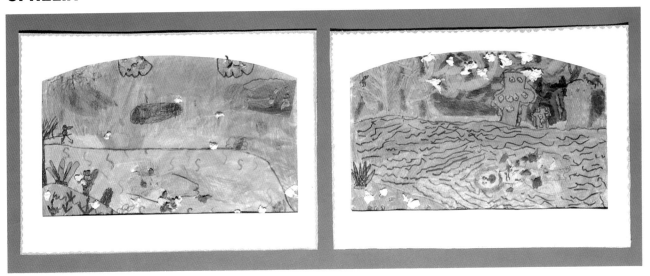

Materials:

White paper for background

Piece of light green tissue paper, the same size as above

Scraps of coloured paper for leaves and flowers, for example, tissue paper, crêpe paper

Thick felt-tip pens or paints

Thin paintbrushes, scissors and glue

1. Spread glue along the edges of the white paper and press the green tissue paper flat on to this.
2. Look at Millais' painting on the facing page, and, using felt-tip pen, draw two lines across the page to show the river banks. Draw the figure in the river.
3. Colour the river and its banks using felt-tip pens in blues and greens, and add other details using scraps.

OPHELIA STORIES

Draw borders around the creative writing and decorate these.

Use felt-tip pens or coloured pencils to draw leaves and flowers.

Mount on green paper and glue on to a background in a different shade of green.

Cut foliage from crêpe paper, tissue paper or other green paper, arrange and glue down.

Make small flowers from coloured paper and add to the display.

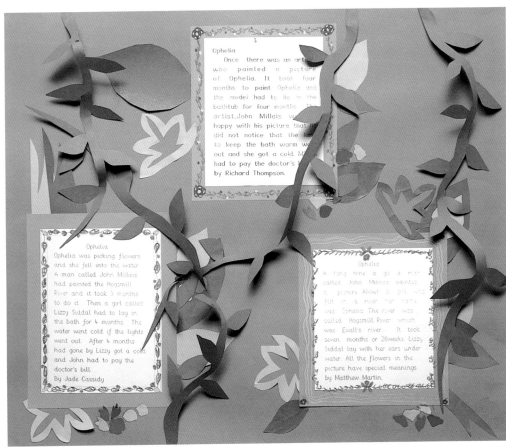

Claude Monet (1840-1926)

Spring, 1886, by Claude Monet (1840-1926), Fitzwilliam Museum, University of Cambridge / Bridgeman Art Library, London

When Claude Monet was five years old, his family moved from Paris to the Port of Le Havre on the Normandy coast. All his life he had a passion for the sea and water in all its forms - sea, rivers, streams and ponds. When he was l6, Monet met an artist called Eugene Boudin when they were both displaying their work in a local picture framer's shop. Boudin encouraged Monet to paint outdoors at a time when most artists painted landscapes in the studio.

When he was young, Monet was poor, and struggled to make money from his paintings. Much later, his paintings began to sell and he became successful and well-known. He moved to Giverny, 40 miles from Paris, and lived there for forty-three years, creating a wonderful garden which was a work of art in itself. He painted hundreds of pictures of it, trying to capture the impression of the moment. He particularly liked to paint the Japanese bridge and the waterlilies in the pond. His garden has been restored, and visitors from all over the world come to see it.

REFLECTIONS

Children's paintings inspired by Monet's *Regatta at Argenteuil*

When Monet lived at Argenteuil, he had a boat converted into a studio which enabled him to paint on the river. *The Regatta at Argenteuil* was probably painted from the studio boat. He loved to paint water with the light sparkling on it, and the landscape reflected in it.

Materials:
Piece of thin card or paper in pale blue
Paint, thickened with strong glue
Pencil
Thin paintbrushes

1. Look at a print of Monet's *Regatta at Argenteuil* and notice which colours he used.
2. Fold the paper to make a horizon line.
3. Using horizontal strokes, paint the water below the fold line. Leave to dry.
4. Paint the sky using the same horizontal technique.
5. Use small dabbing strokes to make the reflections of the buildings and boats in the water.

● Make a list of things you might see near a river, for example, bridge, boats, banks, swans, ducks, etc. Using the technique above, paint the water first, then make it into a scene with these objects, and add reflections.

'MONET CORNER'

The idea of this display is to recreate the atmosphere of the garden at Giverny and to provide a setting for children's artwork. It can be made on a tabletop or on the floor.

- Use green material or paper to make a base. Cut some blue crêpe, foil or any other blue paper, for the pond, and build up the banks using crushed green tissue or crêpe paper.
- Arrange children's artwork on a blue background.
- Make a Japanese bridge using strong card painted green, add waterlilies and fronds (see below).

Waterlilies

Cut out small circles of tissue paper in pink, white and green. Fold the pink and white circles in half and cut points into the outside edge. Open the circles out. Put glue in the middle of a green circle and press a pink and white circle on to this. Add more pointed shapes, gluing each one in the middle. Make the pointed edges stand up to form the flower.

Fronds

Cut a strip from the end of a folded roll of crêpe paper and cut the shape as shown. Open this out, and drape it over a line strung across a corner.

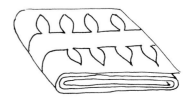

WATERLILY WINDOWS

Materials:
Stiff coloured paper for frame,
   e.g black, blue or dark green
Tissue paper for watery
   background,
   e.g. turquoise, pale green
Scraps of tissue paper in
   assorted colours, e.g. pink,
   green, blue, white - for
   waterlilies and background
   shapes
Piece of white paper, slightly
   smaller than the outside
   edge of the frame
Pastels in pinks, yellows, blues,
   greens
Scissors, glue

1. Cut out a frame from the stiff paper.
2. Cut the tissue paper for the water the same size as the frame. Spread glue carefully on the back of the frame and press the tissue paper on to it, keeping it straight and flat. Leave it to dry. Trim the tissue paper.
3. Make waterlilies (see page 30), leaves, willow branches and, if desired, a bridge, bushes and flowers. Glue on to the tissue paper background to create a water garden.
4. Glue some tissue shapes on to the white paper and decorate the background with pastels.
5. Dab glue on the back of the frame at each corner. Place this on the white paper. Some shapes will appear to be under water.

FLOWERS
Monet created flowery effects by using small separate brush strokes. Experiment with different coloured backgrounds to see which colours give a strong contrast.

1. Using green pastels, create the effect of foliage.
2. Keeping the paintbrush upright, dab first red paint then white paint over the background. There will be shades of pink where the colours overlap.

PASTEL AND PAINT

Using a dabbing movement, create your own Monet-style picture with pastels and paint.

Monet often had to work very quickly to keep pace with changing light and weather conditions. *The Lady with the Parasol* was painted on a windy day with clouds blowing across the sky. *The Poppy Field* shows quick dabs of colour which suggest masses of flowers.

Monet painted *The Poplar Trees* as part of a series. He painted other series on various subjects, for example, haystacks, and Rouen Cathedral. Sometimes he would paint l5 canvases on the same subject, at different times of the day. His stepdaughter, Blanche, carried all his canvases in a wheelbarrow so he could work on each canvas as the light changed.

PICNIC SCENE
Monet loved food, and meals were important family times. He loved painting out of doors and also loved eating out of doors. Picnics occur in many of his pictures.

● Create a picnic in the classroom, using real food and objects. Draw or paint a detail of the scene. Try this from different angles round the room. After the drawing session, have a class picnic. Talk about food from other countries.

PAINTER'S BOX

Materials:
A cardboard box with a lid
Paint, thickened with glue or washing powder, in soft blues, greens and pinks
Brushes - thick and thin
Scraps of tissue and coloured paper for decoration
Felt-tip pens in pastel colours
Scissors, glue

1. Paint the box and lid all over using dabs of paint. Leave to dry, then paint the base last.
2. Decorate with tissue paper.
3. If desired, 'varnish' the box with a mixture of strong glue and water. Leave to dry.
4. Use to display brushes, paints, etc.

● Decorate sheets of tissue paper or white paper with dabs of colour to make wrapping paper. To cover large areas of paper quickly, use sponge dipped in paint.
● Design greeting and gift cards using this paper. Make three-dimensional waterlilies to decorate Monet-style cards.
● Cover small notebooks with this paper to make sketchpads. On small cards, paint miniature versions of Monet paintings. Make your own designs using pastels, coloured pencils and felt-tip pens.
● Make some of the above items based on other artists.

Mary Cassatt (1844-1926)

Mother and Child, by Mary Cassatt (1844-1926), Pushkin Museum, Moscow / Bridgeman Art Library, London

Mary Cassatt came from the United States of America. Her father was a banker who liked travelling around Europe with his family. Cassatt first went to Europe when she was six years old. Her family stayed in Paris until she was eleven. She went to many art exhibitions there and studied French with her brothers and sisters. The family returned to live in America.

Even though it was difficult for women to become artists at this time, Cassatt decided she wanted to paint. Her father was very unhappy about this, but she continued to study art. She travelled between America and Europe, lived in Paris for many years and became famous for her paintings of mothers with their children. Often she painted members of her own family.

Her brother helped her to collect Impressionist paintings and to take them back to the United States. She admired the Japanese prints that she saw in Paris, and many of her pictures show this influence.

CHILDREN AT THE BEACH

Child's picture inspired by a Mary Cassatt painting called *Two children at the Sea-shore,* 1884

This painting shows two little girls playing on the beach, not taking any notice of the artist. The figures fill most of the picture. Try sketching a young child and see how difficult it is to draw people who are constantly moving.

Materials:
Two pieces of paper for background and figures
Paints in blue and yellow
Pastels in blue, white, red and yellow
Scissors, glue

1. Paint a background of sand, sea and sky. Use shades of yellow for the sand, and shades of blue for the water and sky. Leave to dry. Draw boats and rocks with pastels.
2. Draw two children on a separate piece of paper. Colour them, using pastels.
3. Cut them out and glue them on to the background.
4. Find a photograph (or take one yourself) of two children playing. Make your own picture using this as a guide.
5. Make a beach background and add a different subject, for example, picnic, sandcastle, towels.

Georges Seurat (1859-1891)

Georges Seurat was born in Paris. His father was quite wealthy, but was often away from home. Seurat's mother used to take him walking in the pleasure gardens nearby. His uncle, who was very fond of painting, would take him out sketching. When he was fifteen, Seurat went to a local drawing school and, two years later, to the School of Fine Arts. There he learnt all the traditional techniques of art, and grew to love the art of ancient times.

Very little is known of Seurat's life because he was secretive and shy, and his family burnt his papers after he died at the age of 31.

Seurat did not need to sell his pictures to make a living, so he had a lot of time to prepare his big paintings, together with many smaller drawings, studies and paintings. He sketched in the open air in the mornings, and painted in his studio in the afternoons. Each summer, he would take a trip to the coast to paint scenes of the seaside. His friends said he was serious and calm, often silent in a crowd, but he would become excited when talking about his own experiments with techniques of painting.

Sunday Afternoon on the Isle of the Grand Jatte by Georges Pierre Seurat (1859-91), Art Institute of Chicago / Bridgeman Art Library, London

It took Seurat two years to finish this painting. Every day he went to the island of Grande Jatte on the River Seine and sketched the activity around him. Then he came back to the studio and worked on the huge canvas. Look carefully at the picture to find a nurse, soldiers, a monkey and a pug dog. What else can you find in the picture?

FRAME PICTURES

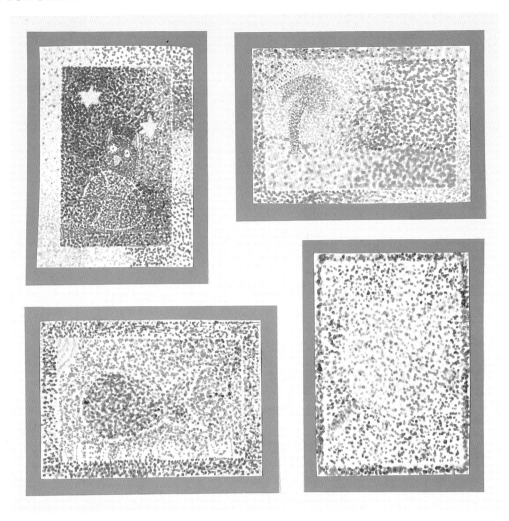

1. Use a pencil to rule a narrow border around the edge of a small piece of paper.
2. Draw some simple outlines lightly with pencil.
3. Fill in the picture with dots of colour using felt-tip pens.
4. Make a border using colours which contrast with those in the picture.

● As it takes a long time to complete a picture using this technique, use small pieces of paper, or work in pairs.

FINGER PRINTING

To introduce young children to pointillism, start with some finger-printing.

1. Cover a sheet of white paper with tissue paper, folding it over on to the back and gluing it down. This makes a good surface for finger-printing.
2. Make a border using several different colours.
3. Finger print a picture in the middle.
4. Fill in the remaining spaces with a contrasting colour.

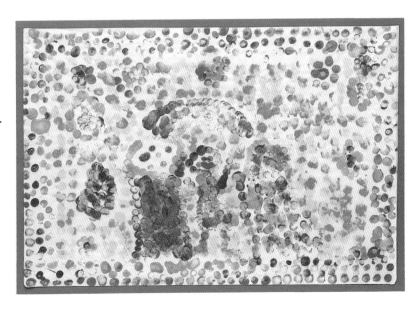

DRAWING WITH DOTS

- Using a felt-tip pen of medium thickness, draw a picture of, for example, a landscape, boats, animals, etc. Place thin paper over the drawing and secure with paperclips. Using black or coloured felt-tip pens, go over the outline with dots.
- Using a pencil, build up a picture with dots. Include a decorative frame made in the same way. Experiment with a variety of drawing implements, for example, ball point pens.

EIFFEL TOWER

In l887-89 the most exciting technological achievement was the building of the Eiffel Tower which was then the tallest man-made structure in the world. In Seurat's painting (and in this child's version of it) the top of the tower is missing. When Seurat painted this picture, the tower was still being built.

- Experiment first by using thick paint and brushes of different thicknesses. Keep the brush at right angles to the picture to apply the paint in small dots.
- Draw a simple shape and cover each area with dots of colour. Use the pointillist technique of placing dots of contrasting colour against each other, for example, blue and yellow to make green.

Vincent van Gogh (1853-1890)

Entrance to the Public Gardens at Arles, by Vincent van Gogh (1853-90), Phillips Collection, Washington D.C. / Bridgeman Art Library, London

Van Gogh often painted pictures of places in the area where he lived. This painting shows the park near the Yellow House where van Gogh lived in Arles. Look at the strong colours, the thick brush strokes and the interesting composition of this painting.

Vincent van Gogh came from a small village in Holland. He became interested in art when he worked for his uncle who was an art dealer. His father was a church minister, and when he was older van Gogh became a preacher for a while. Then he became an artist, and his early paintings such as *The Potato Eaters* used dark and earthy colours. Later he moved to Paris and was influenced by the bright colours which the Impressionists used.

Van Gogh was poor and lonely for most of his life. He struggled with illness but he found some happiness in his belief in God and a sense of joy in painting. This shows in the strong, bold brush-strokes and the bright colours.

He used colour to express feelings rather than to copy the colours in nature. He liked the strong effect of placing complementary or contrasting colours next to each other.

Vincent was encouraged and helped by his loving younger brother, Theo. They wrote many letters to each other, often discussing van Gogh's paintings. Despite Theo's help, van Gogh only sold one painting during his lifetime. Now his paintings are among the most valuable in the world.

DIRECTIONAL LINES

Van Gogh's drawings used directional lines to create a sense of movement.

- Draw a picture using lots of strong separate lines. Van Gogh used pen and ink.
- Try making a picture using any of the following: pencil, felt-tip pens, ballpoint pen, fountain pen, pastels, chalk or charcoal. Experiment with different thicknesses, pressures and types of line (long, short, wavy, curly, swirling, zig-zag) on a spare piece of paper, before drawing the picture.
- After practising these, paint a whole painting with bright colours and strong, directional brushstrokes. To get strong, thick brushstrokes (like an oil-painting), mix glue with the paint. Try using papers of different colours and textures (tissue paper, card, wallpaper, etc.).
- If desired, the painting when dry can be 'varnished' with a glaze of diluted strong glue.

STARRY SKY

Materials:
Large sheets of white paper
Paint, thickened with glue, in blue (medium-dark), yellow and white
Small amount of orange paint
Medium and thick brushes
Wide-toothed comb or cardboard cut into a comb shape
A pencil

1. Look closely at a print of van Gogh's *Starry Night,* and discuss how he has painted the moon and the stars in the sky. Note the direction of the brushstrokes, especially around the stars.
2. Draw large swirling shapes freely across the page using a pencil.
3. Paint the sky around the outside of the swirls. Then use yellow and white paint to sweep around inside the shapes to create moon, stars and clouds.
4. Comb the paint in the direction of the brushstrokes and add touches of orange paint.
● Thick paint can also be moved about using fingers, a round-bladed knife, or pieces of cardboard.

SUNFLOWERS

Sunflowers were special to van Gogh. He painted many pictures of them because he loved their bright colours and spiky shapes.

For this version of a van Gogh sunflower picture, the children decided to use tissue paper, paint and coloured paper. The background was covered with two colours of tissue paper. The flowers were made from layers of tissue petals to create a 3D effect.

LE ZOUAVE

This collage picture is an interpretation of van Gogh's painting *Le Zouave*. Zouaves were French soldiers who wore very bright uniforms. Van Gogh often used the local people as models, for example, the postman and the doctor.

Materials:
A piece of paper for figure
Brightly coloured paper
Paints and brushes
Felt-tip pens
Pencil, scissors and glue

1. Look at a portrait by van Gogh.
2. Make the background first, using any appropriate materials.
3. Draw the figure on paper. Colour and put in the details with pens, paint or pieces of paper.
4. Cut the figure out and glue on to the background.

VAN GOGH'S BEDROOM

Van Gogh wanted to bring lots of artists together to paint. He rented a house he called the 'Yellow House' in Arles, France. Only the painter Gauguin came to join him. This is van Gogh's bedroom in the house.

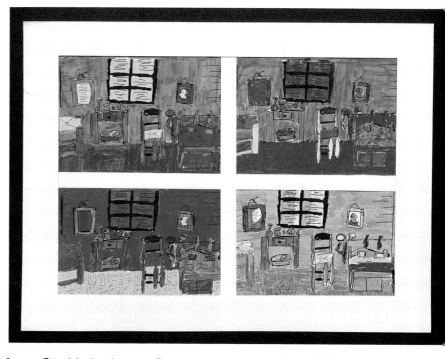

Materials:
A sheet of white photocopy paper cut into quarters
A pencil and thin black pen
Brightly coloured felt-tip pens (no black, brown or grey)

1. Find a line drawing or a painting of van Gogh's bedroom. Draw your own version of this.
2. Make three photocopies and colour all four in a variety of colour schemes, making one the same as van Gogh's bedroom in his painting.

TEXTURED LANDSCAPE

Van Gogh often applied paint very thickly to create a strongly textured surface. This technique is called *impasto*.

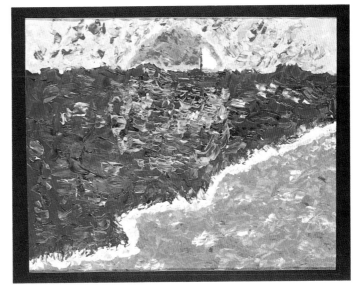

Materials:
White paper for background
Thick paint, mixed with glue in red, yellow, blue and white (in jars)
Thick paint brushes, glue spreaders
Newspaper, pencil

1. Fold some sheets of newspaper to make pads for colour-mixing.
2. Put one brush in each colour and use these to take the paint out and put it on the newspaper pads. Only use the brushes for this purpose, in order to keep the colours pure.
3. Using the glue spreaders, mix colours on the newspaper, not in the pots.
4. Draw a few simple lines on the paper to make a landscape scene, and make a picture using the glue spreaders to dab the paint on. Some colours can be mixed on the picture itself.

ALMOND BLOSSOM

Like other Impressionists, van Gogh was inspired by the Japanese prints which were popular at the time. One painting he did in the Japanese style was of an almond tree (*Almond Blossom,* 1890). He painted this as a gift for his newly born nephew.

Materials:
White paper for background
Turquoise tissue paper - two layers (these should be larger than the white background)
White paper for branches
Boxed tissues (white) or tissue paper
Coloured pencils, scissors and glue

1. Cover the background paper with a layer of turquoise tissue paper, folding the surplus and gluing to the back.
2. Repeat with another layer and turn over.
   Draw three large branches on the white paper. Colour, cut out and glue down on the blue background.
3. Cut lots of circles at once by using several layers of white tissue paper.
4. Place dabs of glue along the branches and press the circles into this to make the blossoms.

Pablo Picasso (1881-1973)

Picasso was born in Spain. His father taught painting and drawing and recognised his son's artistic talent at an early age. When Picasso was only 14, his drawings were so outstanding that he was accepted into the advanced class at the School of Fine Arts in Barcelona. Five years later he moved to Paris where he lived and worked for most of his very long life. He produced thousands of paintings and drawings, many sculptures, pieces of pottery, stage designs and book illustrations. He was always trying out new ideas and painted in many different styles.

PICASSO'S SYMBOL OF PEACE

Picasso was upset by the horrors of war, and he painted pictures such as *Guernica* to show other people how he felt. In 1949, Picasso designed a poster for an International Peace Conference, showing the Dove of Peace. In 1952 he turned an old chapel into a Temple of Peace by painting huge murals showing the triumph of peace over war. Around this time he did many drawings of doves and even named his daughter 'Paloma' (Spanish for 'dove'). Here are two versions of the Peace Dove inspired by Picasso's drawings. Design your own. Keep them simple.

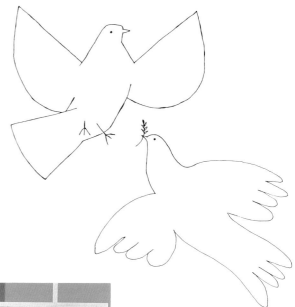

BLUE PERIOD (1901-1904)

At this time, Picasso painted pictures of poor and unhappy people. Picasso showed what they looked like, but also suggested how they felt by using many different shades of blue. Using a mixture of paint and pastel in varying shades of blue, create your own picture.

WOMAN IN A CHAIR

Picasso painted many portraits and made some of them look unusual by distorting and rearranging parts of them. This child's version was created by mixing oil pastels on paper, and was inspired by Picasso's *Woman in a Chair with a Yellow Background* (1937).

Materials:
Coloured paper for background
White paper for figure
Black felt-tip pen
Pencil
Oil pastels
Extra piece of white paper for colour mixing
Scissors, glue

1. Look at a brightly coloured Picasso portrait.
2. Draw your own version or make a copy of the figure using pencil on white paper.
3. Trace over the pencil outline with black felt-tip pen.
4. On the extra piece of paper, experiment with different combinations of colours using the pastels. Put two layers of colour on top of each other and blend lightly with your finger to reproduce the colours used in the picture.
5. Now colour in your own picture.
6. Cut out the figure and glue on to the coloured background.
7. Repeat this colour mixing technique on the background.

PICASSO'S SCULPTURES

Here are some ideas to try:
● Use metal cutlery, nuts, bolts, etc., and Plasticine, to create a 3D sculpture.
● Use pipe-cleaners and papier-mâché to create free-standing people or animals.
● Cut slits in cardboard and slot pieces together to build up an abstract shape.

Paul Klee (1879-1940)

Paul Klee was born in Switzerland but spent most of his life in Germany. When he was young he was gifted at painting, music and writing. His family wanted him to become a musician, but he decided to be an artist. For years he concentrated on drawing before he experimented with colour.

Klee was fascinated by the way lines can create patterns and make pictures. He loved to watch his pen move across the page. Sometimes he used lines to create a sense of space, sometimes to suggest a person, an animal, a tree or a building. He did not think it necessary to draw things as they are. Many of his pictures are imaginative rather than realistic.

Der Orden Von Hohen C. 192I, by Paul Klee, watercolour, pen and ink, Penrose Collection, Burgh Hill House, Chiddingly, East Sussex

This picture includes the features of a face in an unusual way. Klee loved music and he included some musical symbols in the picture. Look carefully and see what else it suggests.

● Create a face using other shapes, and experiment with a variety of media.

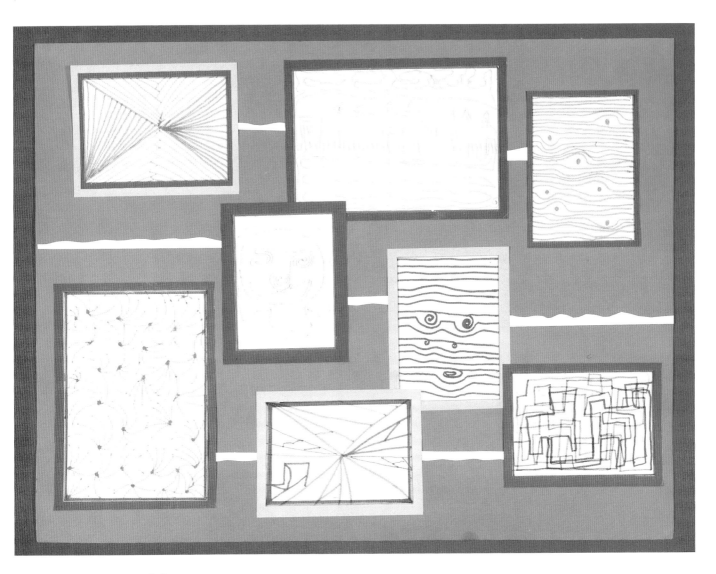

LINE DRAWINGS

Some of Klee's line drawings were made by creating a rule (see below) and seeing what happened when he followed it. Try these rules:

● OBSTACLE RACE (top right and middle right)
  Draw some obstacles - dots, little squares, or other small shapes, placed at random all over the paper. Avoiding the obstacles, draw horizontal lines from one side of the paper to the other. Do not let any lines touch. Try changing the colours, the size of the obstacles, or the thickness of the lines.
● A CHANGE OF DIRECTION (bottom right)
  Draw a continuous line which travels all over the paper, changing colour and direction as it goes. The line should be straight and make only right-angled turns. Eventually it should join up with itself at the point where it started.
● CURVES AND POINTS (bottom left)
  Draw a dot anywhere on the paper with curving lines radiating from it in the same direction. Using the end of one of the curving lines as a new centre, draw lines radiating from that point. Repeat the process to cover the page.
● THE UNBROKEN LINE (top middle and middle left)
  Start a line at the bottom of the page and, without taking the pen or pencil off the paper, draw a landscape or townscape. Do not let the line cross over itself. Also try this technique to create a strange face.

Use some of the ideas above to create your own rule for drawing. Now make this into a picture. A child has drawn the picture, top left, to demonstrate this.

CITYSCAPE

Klee often built up drawings from small repeated patterns, creating weird plants, hanging lanterns or strange cityscapes. Try using these patterns below (or invent your own) to build your cityscape. Cut the buildings out in a long strip. Glue on to a coloured background and decorate with felt-tip pens.

Paul Klee was well-known both as an artist and a teacher or art. He encouraged his students to experiment with the effects of colour, as he did himself all his life. He often used only a few colours so that they would have a stronger effect.

PAINT AND PRINT (top picture)
This is a child's version of an original. Paint blocks of colour to cover a piece of paper. When dry, draw abstract shapes on this background. Fill in these new shapes with dots of thick paint, printed with the blunt end of a pencil.

ABSTRACT LINES (bottom picture)
Draw some black lines with crayon on a piece of coloured paper. Use paint in different shades of one colour, leaving space around the lines to let the background show.

SPONGE PRINT
Sponge print a background in pastel colours. Leave to dry. Draw lines and shapes on top with thick black felt-tip pens.

TEXTURED SURFACE
Rub over a textured surface - wallpaper or corrugated card - using the side of a crayon or pastel with the wrappers removed (in reds or browns). Draw shapes on top of this background using a black pastel or charcoal.

THE FOREST IN AUTUMN
Paul Klee usually invented titles for his paintings after he had finished them.

Make a list of colours which make you think of each of the four seasons. Using paper in the colours chosen for one season, make the picture first and then think of a title to go with it, for example, *Autumn Wind, The Forest in Autumn, Falling Leaves.*

Materials:
A piece of coloured paper for the background
Scraps of paper in chosen colours
Glue (scissors optional)

1. Tear (or cut) the scraps of paper into small shapes.
2. Spread glue over the background and cover with the torn shapes, making most of them overlap.
3. Mount the picture using one of the chosen colours.
4. Glue the title on to the frame.

René Magritte (1898-1967)

René Magritte was a surrealist painter who lived and worked in Belgium. One thing all surrealist painters have in common is that their paintings look very unusual. Magritte liked to paint ordinary objects in a realistic style but he looked for different ways to make them seem extraordinary and magical. Although his paintings looked strange, he seemed very ordinary himself, leading a quiet married life in a Belgian town. His life consisted of routines - every day he walked his dog, Lulu, to the shops and every afternoon he went to the village and played chess. He dressed very like the bowler-hatted man who appears in many of his paintings.

A Surreal Display

In Magritte's paintings, objects appear in odd places and in strange combinations. To make the display above, cover a box with sky-patterned paper and brick-patterned paper for the background. Combine cut-out pictures of objects and figures found in Magritte paintings with real objects, for example, bowler hats, pipes, apples, combs, chairs, fish, etc.

● Make a 3D display with other objects and with different backgrounds.

MAKING CHANGES

Here are some of the ways that Magritte made ordinary objects look strange and funny

Changing the size of things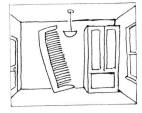

Changing the place of things

Changing the texture of things

Changing parts of things

Try changing the background, the colour, the shape, or the behaviour of an object.

UNLIKELY COMBINATIONS

Make a list of everyday objects and animals - apple, door, flower, cup, egg, hat, moon, television, teapot, dog, wheel, fork, cat, fish. Have fun combining two of these to make an unusual picture.

Draw with pencil first, then colour with felt-tip pens or paint.

THE BOWLER-HATTED MAN

Draw the outline of the head and shoulders of the man on black paper, using a pencil. Carefully cut out this shape. Use a piece of coloured paper, larger than the cut-out shape, and decorate it. Then place it under the black paper with the missing shape, and glue down.

STRANGE HEADS

Look at *The Man in the Bowler Hat*. Draw a picture of the shoulders and head only, leaving the face blank. Draw a collar and tie and colour them with pastels. Cut this out and glue on to a background. Draw and colour a bird. Cut it out and glue on to the face. You can make your own version by using different objects in place of the bird.

● In the photograph above, one head is replaced by a pear. Try this with other fruits or vegetables.
● In one of Magritte's paintings there are many bowler-hatted men apparently floating in mid-air. Make your own picture using this idea.
● Draw a bowler-hatted man and place him in an unusual scene, for example, underwater, in a fire, on a mountain top.

LANDSCAPE FACES
These children's pictures were inspired by Magritte's painting, *Faces in a Landscape.*

Materials:
White paper, and magazines to cut out
Scissors and glue

1. Look through the magazines for a photograph of a landscape. Cut it out and glue on to white paper.
2. Find eyes, nose, and other parts of a face to glue on to the landscape.
● Experiment with a variety of backgrounds for the faces - sky, sea, hills, rocks, gardens.

BIRD'S NEST
This is a version of Magritte's painting, *Spring.*

Materials:
White paper
Magazines to cut up
Scissors and glue

1. Find a picture of sky to use as background. Cut out and glue on to white paper.
2. Look through the magazines for some pictures of foliage - trees, bushes, reeds, etc.
3. Cut out some foliage and glue on to the lower part of the sky to make the foreground.
4. Cut the shape of a bird out of foliage, and glue to the background.
5. Add a nest from other cut-out pieces.

David Hockney (1937-   )

David Hockney grew up in the industrial town of Bradford in the north of England. A lot of the buildings were of stone, made even darker by the smoke from the factory chimneys. The weather was often cold and rainy. When he finished art school in London he decided to move to the United States of America. He enjoyed living there and he loved the bright sunny weather in California. Many of his paintings are also bright and sunny, with strong clear colours.

When Hockney was a boy, his father often took him to the theatre, which he loved. Later, when he became a famous artist, he was asked to design sets and costumes for a number of operas, for example, The Magic Flute. In order to see what his designs would look like, he made miniature theatres. Here is one way of making a simple theatre.

MODEL THEATRE
Materials:
2 large sheets of strong cardboard
Cereal packet - strengthened at the ends to
    maintain box shape
Strong glue and scissors

1. Cut a stage opening from one piece of cardboard.
2. Draw and cut a rectangular hole from each of the larger sides of the cereal box (to let light through).
3. Glue the cereal box, edge on, between the two sheets of card.
4. This forms the structure of the theatre. Paint and decorate as desired.
5. Make a stage set mounted on a piece of card, the width of the cereal box.
6. Find a way to light the set from above.

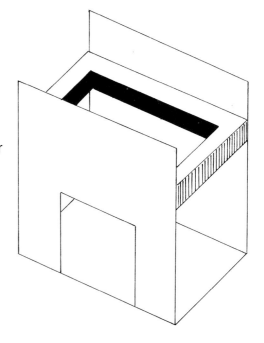

STAGE SET (see facing page)

Design your own stage set for a pantomime or play. Draw or paint a picture to use as a backdrop. Glue this on to the side of a box and stand it up at the back of the set. Draw and colour pictures on rectangles of card to make the wings to go at the sides. Draw and colour figures, making them stand up. Toy models could also be used.

STORMY LANDSCAPE

The picture below was inspired by David Hockney's painting called *Iowa*.

Materials:
White paper for background
Smaller sheets of white paper
Paint in blues and greens, black and white
Large paint brushes
Scissors and glue

1. Combine some of the paints above to make stormy colours.
2. Paint the smaller sheets of paper in these colours and leave to dry.
3. Cut out shapes of trees, clouds, buildings etc. to make a stormy scene.
4. Glue these on to the white background.

● Use this technique to create other scenes, for example, sunset, underwater, Autumn day.
● Print sheets of paper using pieces of sponge, cardboard rolls, polystyrene blocks, etc. Cut these up to make into an abstract pattern.

POOL PICTURES

Many of David Hockney's friends had swimming pools and he often painted pictures of these. He was fascinated by different ways of painting the movement of water in the sunlight. Some of his pictures show a splash of water after someone has dived into the pool.

POOL PICTURE 1

Draw a continuous line on white paper without lifting the pencil off the page, making curves and loops. Trace over this with felt-tip pen and colour in the shapes to make a watery effect. Glue this on to blue paper and decorate.

POOL PICTURE 2

Cover white paper with blue tissue paper. Cut curved shapes of tissue paper in blues and greens to make the patterns on the water, and glue down. Add coloured paper for the poolside.

POOL PICTURE 3

Materials:

Piece of blue paper for background, and smaller piece of paper

Paints in blues and green, paintbrushes

Scraps of brown and green paper, scissors and glue

1. Paint a wavy pattern using blue paints on the smaller paper. Leave to dry.
2. Cut out plant shapes from brown and green paper.
3. Paint green waves on top of the blue. While the paint is still wet, use the other end of the paintbrush to make small wavy patterns.
4. When dry, glue the pool and the plant shapes on to the background.

Hockney liked to paint pictures of objects in bright sunlight. Think of some other subjects suitable for this, for example, beach ball, sunglasses, sun hat. Show the shadows cast by each object.

UMBRELLA
Materials:
Blue card/paper for background
Coloured paper in yellow, red, blue, green
Yellow crêpe paper, larger than width of background paper
A straw or strip of paper for umbrella shaft
Crayons, or pastels, in blues
Scissors and glue

1. Spread glue over the lower half of the blue background paper.
2. Place the crêpe paper on the glued surface and push the paper around to create a crinkled effect.
3. Fold the surplus paper on to the back and glue down.
4. Place the pieces of coloured paper on top of each other and cut a triangle shape. Glue the triangles down to make the umbrella.
6. Draw details with crayons.

PHOTO-MONTAGE
David Hockney is famous for his photo-montage pictures which used hundreds of photographs to create a bigger picture. Make a photo-montage using pictures from magazines and old photographs.

Find magazine pictures in shades of green, and photographs of grass. Cut these into pieces and glue on to a piece of card, overlapping as you go. Cut out animals to place on the grassy background.

● Choose other backgrounds, for example, sea, sky, desert.

Colour

THE PRIMARY COLOURS are the three basic colours - RED, BLUE and YELLOW. They cannot be made by mixing other colours.

THE SECONDARY COLOURS are the three colours that can be made by mixing two of the primary colours - PURPLE, GREEN and ORANGE.

THE COMPLEMENTARY COLOUR of each primary colour is a combination of the other two. For example, the complementary colour of RED is GREEN (a mixture of blue with yellow) and the complementary colour of BLUE is ORANGE (a mixture of red with yellow). This can be seen on a colour wheel (see below), where the complementary colours are opposite each other.

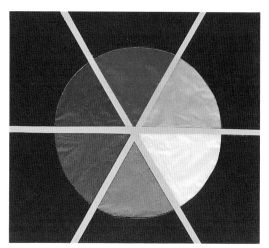

TISSUE COLOUR WHEEL
Materials:
Sheet of black paper
3 pieces of tissue paper (one each of red, blue, yellow), placed on top of each other
Sheet of thin white paper
Small plate or circle template of similar size
Scissors, glue

1. Draw a circle in the middle of the black paper using a small plate. Draw another circle slightly smaller inside this one.
2. Push the points of the scissors through the middle of the black paper and carefully cut out the smaller circle. Turn paper over so that pencil marks do not show.
3. Place the plate on top of the three sheets of tissue paper. Draw round it and cut three circles together. Cut these in half to make semi-circles.
4. Using three of these semi-circles, overlap them with a dab of glue to form a colour wheel with six equal segments. Start with blue and red, then place the yellow one on top. It is important to do them in this order to make a more effective orange and green.
5. Glue the black paper on to the colour wheel. Display on the window.

PRIMARY COLOUR MIXING
This is a simple way for younger children to learn colour mixing. Try this on scraps of paper first and only mix two colours to start with, for example, yellow and blue, red and yellow, before trying it with three colours.

Materials:
White paper. Red, yellow and blue paint
Wide glue spreader
1. Place a spoonful of each colour in the centre of the paper.
2. Holding the spreader vertically, draw the paint from the centre to the edges of the paper.
3. Repeat this to cover the paper.

ARTIST'S PALETTE

Materials:

Black and brown paper for brushes
Coloured paper for palette and
    background
6 round shapes in red, yellow, blue,
    green, purple and orange
Brown crayon without wrapper
Scissors and glue

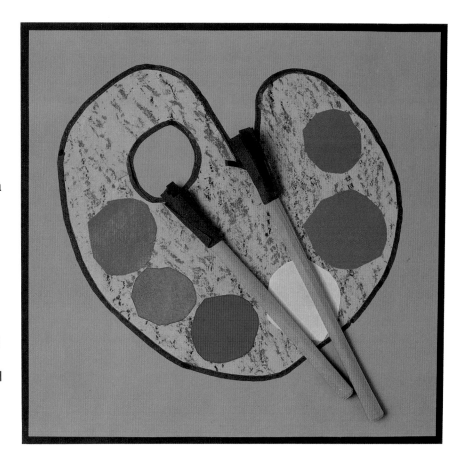

1. Draw a palette shape and cut out a
   circle for the thumb. Cut out the
   palette.
2. Holding the palette against a
   textured wooden surface, for
   example, table or tree trunk, rub
   over with the side of the crayon.
3. Glue the six colours around the
   edge of the palette.
4. Glue the palette on to the coloured
   background.
5. Cut the brown paper into strips, roll
   and glue into narrow tubes. Make
   a strip of fringed black paper to
   make the 'brushes'.

TORN LINES IN SECONDARY COLOURS

Try this using other colours,
for example, Primary and
Complementary

Materials:

Piece of white paper
Pieces of tissue paper in
    orange, green and purple,
    larger than the white paper
Pieces of gummed paper in
    orange, green or purple

1. Spread glue along the
   edges of the white paper.
2. Place the white paper, glue
   side up, in the middle of the
   tissue paper. Fold the
   surplus tissue paper on to
   the glued edges.
3. Turn paper over and draw
   two or three lines across
   the page.
4. Spread glue along one of
   the lines.
5. Tear one of the gummed papers in to small pieces and place these along the glued line, close to
   each other. Change the colours as you move along the line.
6. Repeat along the other lines.

PAINTED COLOUR CIRCLE

This is another easy way to learn about colour mixing, as there are only two colours involved.

Materials:

Large circle of white paper, divided into eight sections
Black paper circle, larger than the white circle
Strips of black paper
One container of red paint
One container of white paint
Thin brushes
Scissors and glue

1. Paint one segment red and the one next to it white.
2. Add a small amount of red paint to the white container and mix well. Use this to paint the section next to the white one. Add more red paint to the container and paint the third section. Repeat this process round the wheel until each section is painted.
3. When dry, glue on to the black circle and glue the black strips across the wheel.
4. Try this with other colour combinations.

FANTASY LANDSCAPES

This is a colour mixing exercise - so use some of the primary colour paints to mix the secondary colours before starting.

Materials:

Paints in red, yellow, blue
Paints in green, purple and orange (mixed from previous three colours)
White paper for background
Thick and thin paint brushes

1. Paint a landscape in unexpected colours, for example, purple sun, red grass, green clouds.
2. Use this idea to create other improbable scenes, for example, try combining a seascape, a townscape and a jungle.

COMPLEMENTARY COLOUR BOXES

Find pairs of complementary colours by looking at those opposite each other on a colour wheel.
RED and GREEN   YELLOW and PURPLE   BLUE and ORANGE

MAGAZINE COLLAGE PICTURE
1. Look through magazines and cut out coloured objects or shapes in one of the pairs of complementary colours.
2. Glue these pieces on to a piece of paper to cover the whole area.
3. Make two mounts for this picture - one larger than the other in the same colours as above.
4. Glue the magazine abstract picture on to the smaller mount, then on to the larger mount.

● Look at advertisements and note which colours are used most frequently. Design some advertisements. Try out the three pairs of complementary colours to see which are the most eye-catching.
● Cut up clothing catalogues and make pictures which show the complementary pairs. Design your own outfits in purple and yellow, OR red and green, OR blue and orange.

TO MAKE A DISPLAY
1. Cover some boxes with tissue paper in some of the complementary colours. Add the above pictures.
2. Collect objects in the pairs of colours to create a display, for example, fruit, toys, flowers, felt-tip pens, coloured paper, etc.
3. Arrange the display on a table or in a corner.

COLOUR RUBBINGS

This is a simple method of colour mixing, using crayons instead of paints.

Materials:

Thin paper for background

Small pieces of cardboard - textured if possible

Crayons, with wrappers removed, in blue, yellow and red

1. Cut out a small shape from the cardboard and cut a hole in the centre.
2. Hold the shape underneath the thin paper and rub over it carefully with the side of a crayon, for example, yellow.
3. Keep it in exactly the same place and rub over with another primary colour, for example red, to make orange.
4. Repeat using other colour combinations and make a pattern to cover the page.

COLOUR ABSTRACTS

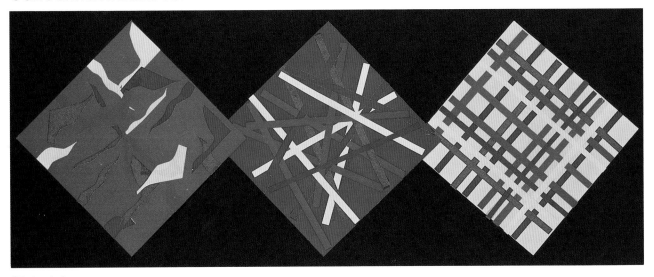

Materials:

Squares of coloured paper in red, yellow, blue, green, purple and orange

Scissors, glue

1. Cut some of the squares into strips.
2. Choose several strips of each of the six colours and glue down on to a coloured square to make a pattern, covering the background paper.
3. Hold several sheets of paper together and cut out an abstract shape. Repeat with the six colours above. Glue these down to make a design.

Faces

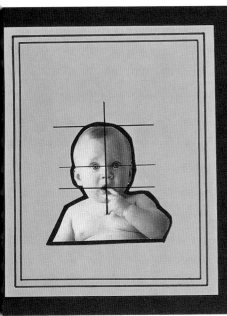  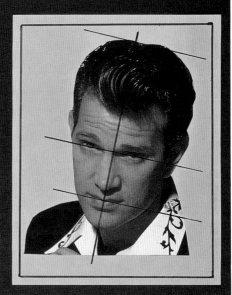

Artists throughout the centuries have been fascinated by the human face and the many variations of feature and expression possible within the basic shape and proportions.

PROPORTIONS

This is a way of finding out about the proportions of the human face. Magazines, newspapers and photographs all provide resources for experimenting.

1. Draw a line from the top of the head, down the middle to the chin.

2. Draw a line across the face through the eyes.

3. Draw a line across the face through the mouth.

● How far down the central line is the line for the eyes?

● Where does the mouth come?

● Look at the proportions of babies', children's and adults' faces.

EXPRESSIONS

● Look at faces in famous paintings. Discuss their expressions and try to imitate them. Use a mirror, if possible, and draw the expressions on your own face.

● Draw as many expressions as you can, for example, angry, sad, puzzled, etc., and label them.

Space and Distance

There are many ways to suggest distance in a picture. Here are four of them.

A. Position on the page
B. Overlapping
C. High and low horizon
D. Size of objects

POSITION ON THE PAGE (picture at top left)
A person or object looks further away if it is higher on the page than another one, even if they are the same size.

OVERLAPPING (picture at rop right)
A person or object partly hidden by another appears to be further away.

HIGH AND LOW HORIZON (picture at bottom left)
The horizon line is where the land and sky appear to meet - and which can only be seen if there are no hills, trees of buildings in the way.

- If you are close to the ground, the horizon line will appear low and objects will stand out against the sky (see first picture of the sailing boat).
- If you are high up (on a building or a hill), the horizon will appear high, and most objects will appear below the horizon (see second picture of the sailing boat).

SIZE OF OBJECTS (picture at bottom right)
Objects look smaller if they are further away. Draw and cut out three people or objects in three sizes. Place them on the background so that it looks as if the smallest one is furthest away. This will create a greater sense of distance and space in the picture.

Perspective

The following ideas are intended as a simple introduction to the use of perspective (see Glossary) to create a sense of space and distance.

PARALLEL LINES

● Discuss the idea of parallel lines. Look around the room and observe that the top and bottom of a window are parallel, and the lines where the wall meets the ceiling and the floor are parallel. Draw some of these lines.

● Glue a picture of a room or building viewed at an angle (estate agents' magazines are useful for this) to a larger piece of paper. Using a ruler, extend the parallel lines in the room or on the building. What happens to the parallel lines in the picture? Draw the parallel lines until they meet, which may be off the picture.

A PERSPECTIVE PICTURE

PICTURE 1 (top left)
● Draw the front of a house in pencil. Draw horizontal and parallel lines through various parts of the picture (for example, top of roof, top and bottom of windows, bottom of wall).
● Draw a vertical line at the side of the house and place a dot at each place where the lines cross.

PICTURE 2 (top right)
● Copy the line with the dots on to the right hand side of another piece of paper.
● Draw a dot on the left hand side of the paper.
● Draw faint pencil lines from this dot to each of the dots on the line, as in the photograph.
● Draw the building within these lines and repeat for more buildings.

PICTURE 3 (bottom)
● Place a dot in the middle of a piece of paper. Repeat the above process on both sides of the picture to create a street scene.
● Make into a picture using coloured paper and felt-tip pens.

Figures

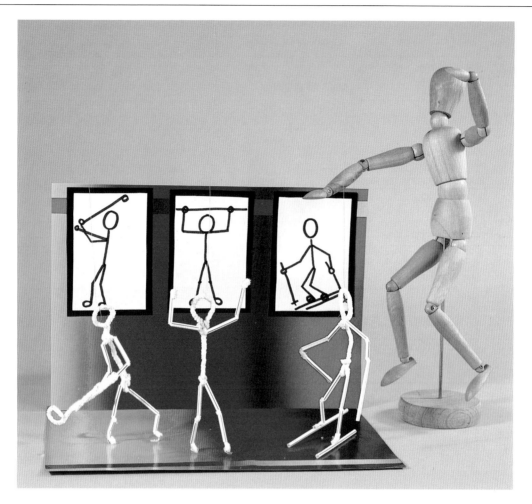

Artists often use wooden manikins to work out proportions and poses of people in their pictures. A simple version can be made using pipe-cleaners and straws. Use three pipe-cleaners for each figure.

Pipe-cleaner 1. Wind one end around a finger and twist to make a head.
Pipe-cleaner 2. Place this across the neck and twist the two ends to make the arms.
Pipe-cleaner 3. Bend in the middle to make the legs and join it on to the body.

Cut straws into short pieces and use two for each limb. Bend the ends to make hands and feet. Figures can be decorated for themes, for example, circus, sport, theatre.

Make drawings of the figures you have made and place them beside the models.

FOR OLDER CHILDREN
● Compare the proportions of figures in magazines. Cut out a figure and use a piece of paper to mark the size of the head. Use this to see how many times the head fits into the total height, for example 1:5, 1:7.
● Using the proportion 1:6, make a Plasticine statue. The head is one unit, the body is two units, and the legs are three units. Try other proportions to make a figure.
● Make different sorts of figures: gladiators, robots, clowns.
● Make marionettes and other jointed puppets. Thread beads on to pipe-cleaners.
● Use pipe-cleaner figures to mimic the poses of famous statues and figures in paintings.
● Collect postcards of paintings with interesting movements and poses.

Movement

Cut out figures from magazines and newspapers showing a variety of sports, for example, footballers, runners, tennis players, hurdlers, skaters, dancers, swimmers, divers.

- Make a collage of figures to show a variety of movements.
- Draw a dot on each joint and link the dots with straight lines to show the movement. Copy the lines and dots of one figure and draw your own person in this pose.

Cut out pictures from magazines which show animals moving.

- Draw a dot on each joint and draw lines to join the dots.
- Copy the shapes of the animals. Make them into realistic pictures or cartoons.
- Write about how different animals move, for example, lions, horses, birds, dogs and cats.

Other Ideas

Making games. Invent a game based on famous artists. It can be a board game, a card game, or a matching game.

Using postcards. Classify these according to subject, for example, portraits, periods of time, costume, transport, time of day. Cover a box and use this for storing postcards. Make suitable dividers.

Jigsaws. Use two small identical pictures. Cut one into pieces to make a jigsaw, and glue the other on to a decorated box. Keep the pieces inside the box.

Colour Flick-book. Fold eight small pieces of paper, which are the same size, to make a flick-book. Colour the edges from blue to yellow, or red to blue. Flick them quickly to see the colour change.

Art folders. Design your own folder to store your pictures in. Decorate with ideas from various artists.

Other Suggestions.
- Collect objects which show works of art, for example, placemats, T-shirts, card packs. Make your own designs for any of these.
- Make a collection of objects which show your interests, for example, sport, reading, toys, games. Draw a portrait of yourself (using a mirror) with your possessions.

Music and Art

1. Some painters (Paul Klee, for example) have tried to capture the mood of a piece of music in a painting and have given their pictures musical names - for example, *Nocturne, Prelude, Symphony.*

● Listen to three or four pieces of music expressing different moods. Choose one and paint a picture which matches the mood of the music. You can listen to the music again, while painting your picture.

2. Some musicians have tried to capture the mood of a painting in a piece of music. The most famous example of this is Modeste Mussorgsky's *Pictures at an Exhibition.* The music describes walking around the gallery and looking at the pictures. As the visitor stops in front of each painting the music represents what is in the picture.

● Draw or paint your idea of what each painting might have looked like. You may need to listen to some of the sections more than once.
● Frame your pictures and set up an exhibition. Invite your friends from other classes for an 'opening'. Provide juice and play the music in the background.

3. Artists who design sets and costumes for ballets, musicals and operas have to think about what is needed for the story, and also listen carefully to the music so that their designs match the style and mood of the music.

● Read the story of a ballet, opera or musical. Listen to some music from each act or scene and design appropriate stage sets and costumes. Your first designs should be on paper, but when you have decided (either individually or in a group) on a design, you can make a model stage set to fit the model theatre described on page 54.
Suggestions for suitable music: *Hansel and Gretel* by Engelbert Humperdinck, *L'Enfant et Les Sortileges* by Maurice Ravel, *The Magic Flute* by W.A. Mozart, *Oliver* by Lionel Bart.

4. People playing musical instruments occur in many paintings (for example, Brueghel's *The Wedding Party* (bagpipes), Watteau's *Fête-champêtre* (guitar).
Find some more paintings with musicians or musical instruments in them. Draw details from them. Cut them out and make a collage - 'A History of Music in Art'.

5. Many musical instruments have interesting shapes. Invent and draw your own unusual musical instruments on card. Find a way to make it produce a sound, for example, by adding elastic bands, pieces of string and small pieces of card.

Glossary

ABSTRACT ART - pictures or sculptures which create an effect using line, shape or colour but do not represent anything recognisable.

CARTOON - originally a drawing made in preparation for a large painting or tapestry. One method of transferring a cartoon to a picture was to prick the outline with a pin and then to rub a pouncing bag (which contained powdered charcoal) over the picture. The black powder left small dots which could then be joined up.

CHARCOAL - a drawing stick made from charred wood.

ENGRAVING - a picture produced by printing:

Line engraving: a print made from a metal plate. The design is cut directly into the metal plate.

Wood engraving: a print made from a block of wood. With this technique, the lines are not cut into the block. The wood is cut away, leaving the lines standing.

ETCHING - a design is cut into a wax coating on a metal plate. The plate is then submerged in acid. This eats into the metal where the wax has been removed. The wax is cleaned off and the plate is printed.

EXPRESSIONISM - a style of art which exaggerates or distorts shape, line and colour, to portray the artistic feelings.

FRESCO - a method of painting a picture on a plaster wall while the plaster is still wet. The painting becomes part of the wall.

GLAZE - a thin layer of transparent paint applied over a picture to create subtle effects.

HATCHING - an effect of shading created by drawing thin lines close together. A darker shade can be achieved by cross-hatching, combining two directions of closely spaced lines.

IMPASTO - paint applied very thickly so that the marks made by brush or palette-knife are clearly visible.

IMPRESSIONISM - style of painting begun by a group of French artists at the end of the 19th Century. The bright colours are applied freely to capture the effects of light.

LINO CUT - a printing technique in which the design is cut into a thick piece of linoleum.

LOGGIA - a room or porch, usually with arches or columns, open to the air.

MONTAGE - a way of making pictures by mounting cut-out illustrations on a backing sheet. It differs from collage in that only ready-made images are used.

PERSPECTIVE - a method of creating a sense of space and distance in a picture. (See page 65.)

PHOTOMONTAGE - a collage using photographs.

POINTILLISM - a painting technique using separate small dots which merge in the eye when viewed from a distance. This effect is called optical mixing, because instead of the colour being mixed before painting, the resulting colour only comes into being when the dots of pure colour are put together in the eye of the viewer.

SURREALISM - An art movement which stressed the importance of the irrational and the subconscious. Surrealistic paintings usually look very strange and often disturbing.

TONDO - a circular painting or relief carving.

WASH - in watercolour painting, a thin, diluted coat of paint applied over a large area.

Woodcut by Cristoforo Coriolano, from Vasari's *Vite*, 1568

For details of further Belair Publications
please write to:
BELAIR PUBLICATIONS LTD
P.O. Box 12, TWICKENHAM, TW1 2QL, England

For sales and distribution (outside USA and Canada)
FOLENS PUBLISHERS
Albert House, Apex Business Centre,
Boscombe Road, Dunstable, Bedfordshire, LU5 4RL
England

For sales and distribution in North America and South America
INCENTIVE PUBLICATIONS
3835 Cleghorn Avenue, Nashville, Tn 37215, U.S.A.

For sales and distribution in Australia EDUCATIONAL SUPPLIES PTY LTD
8 Cross Street, Brookvale, N.S.W. 2100
AUSTRALIA